Traditional Tattoo

Coloring Book

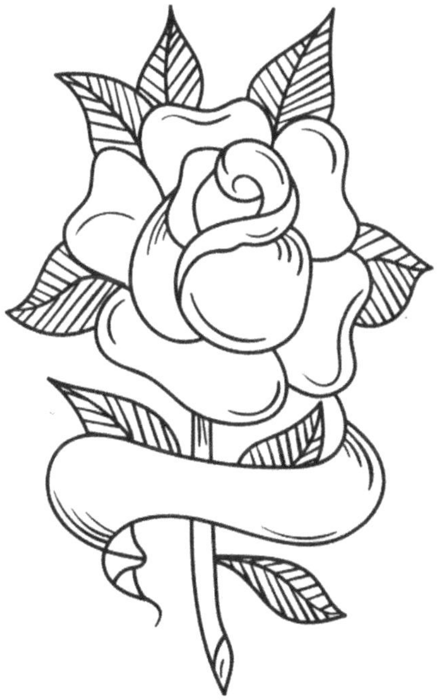

By Bruno Rodriguez

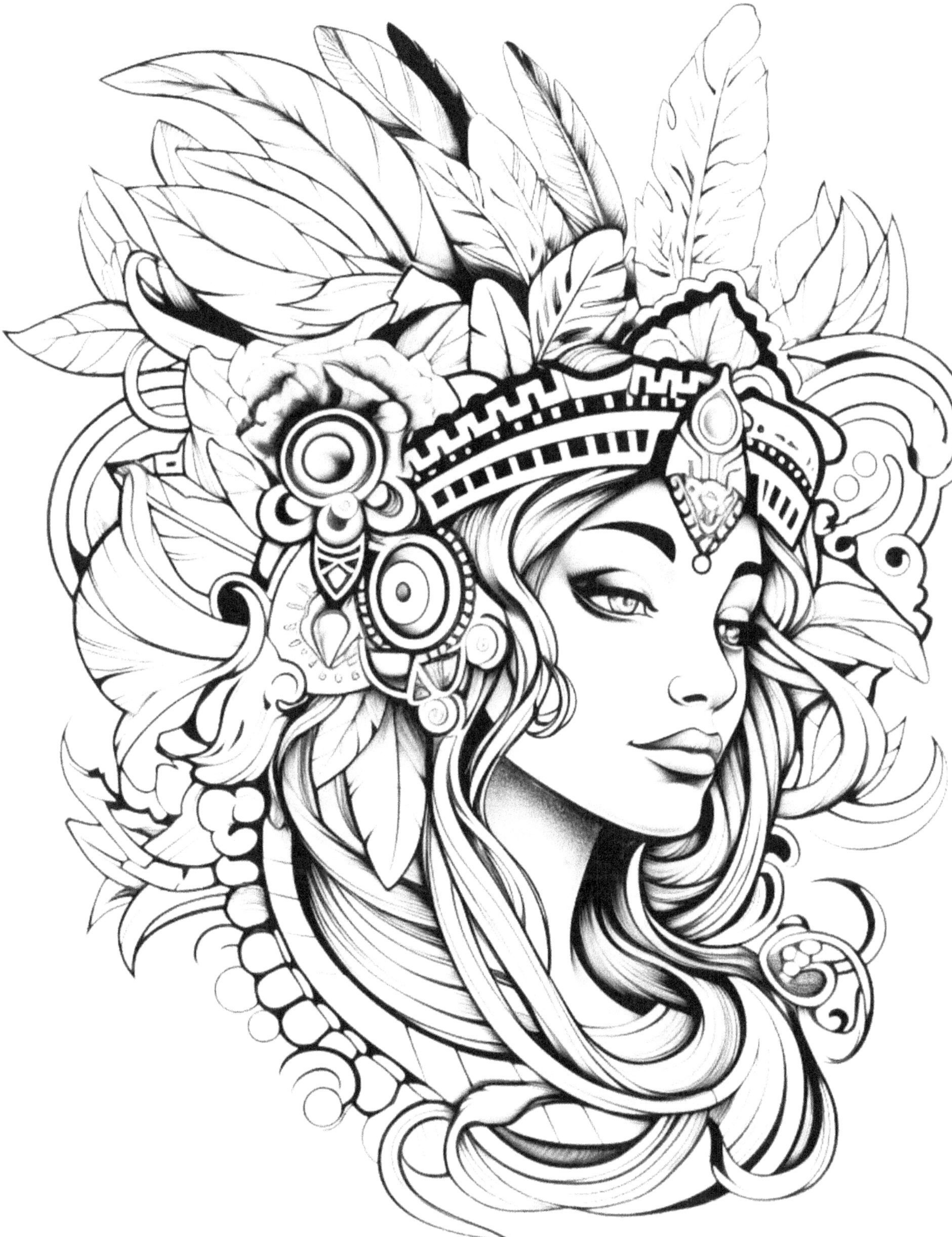

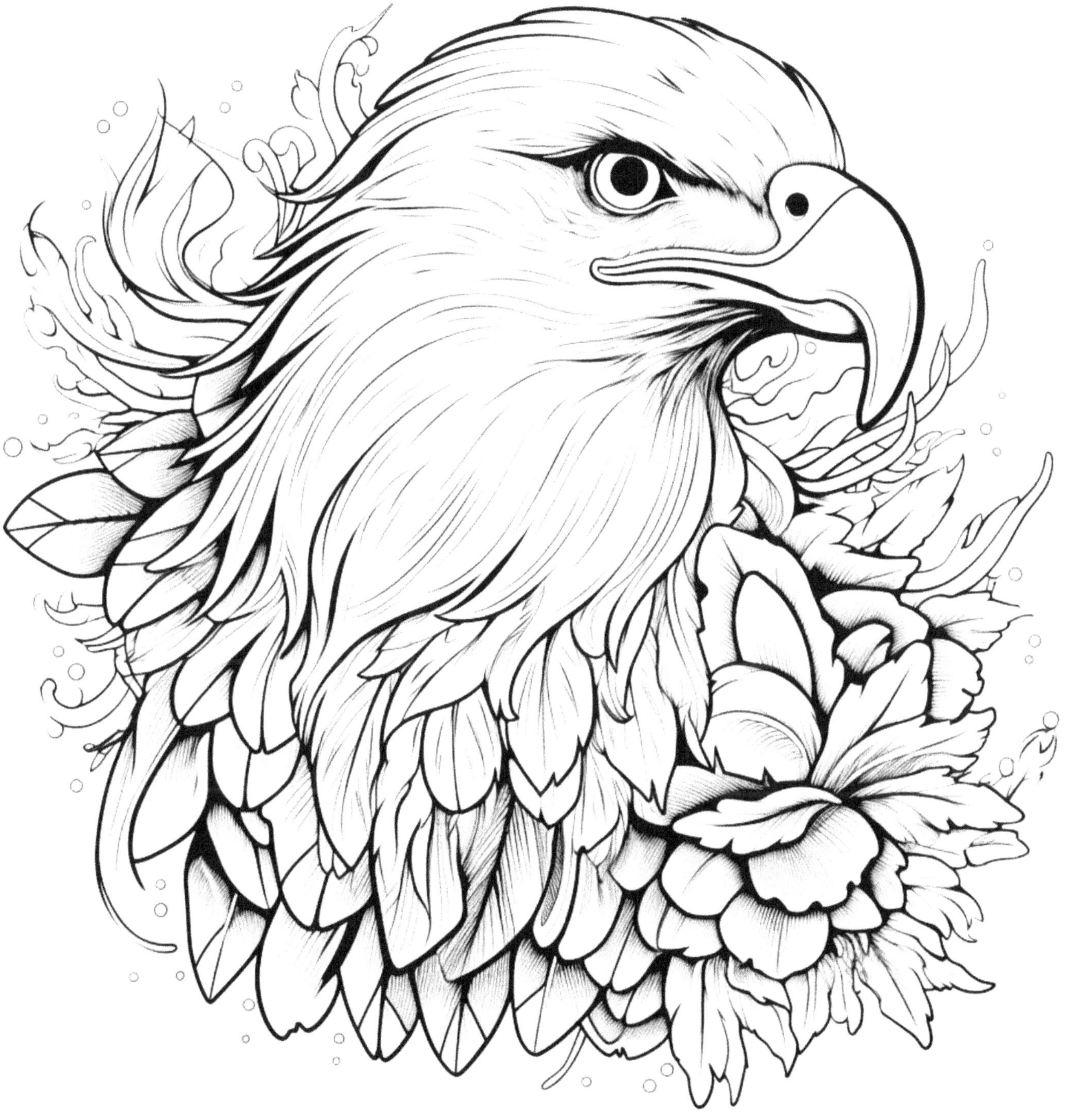

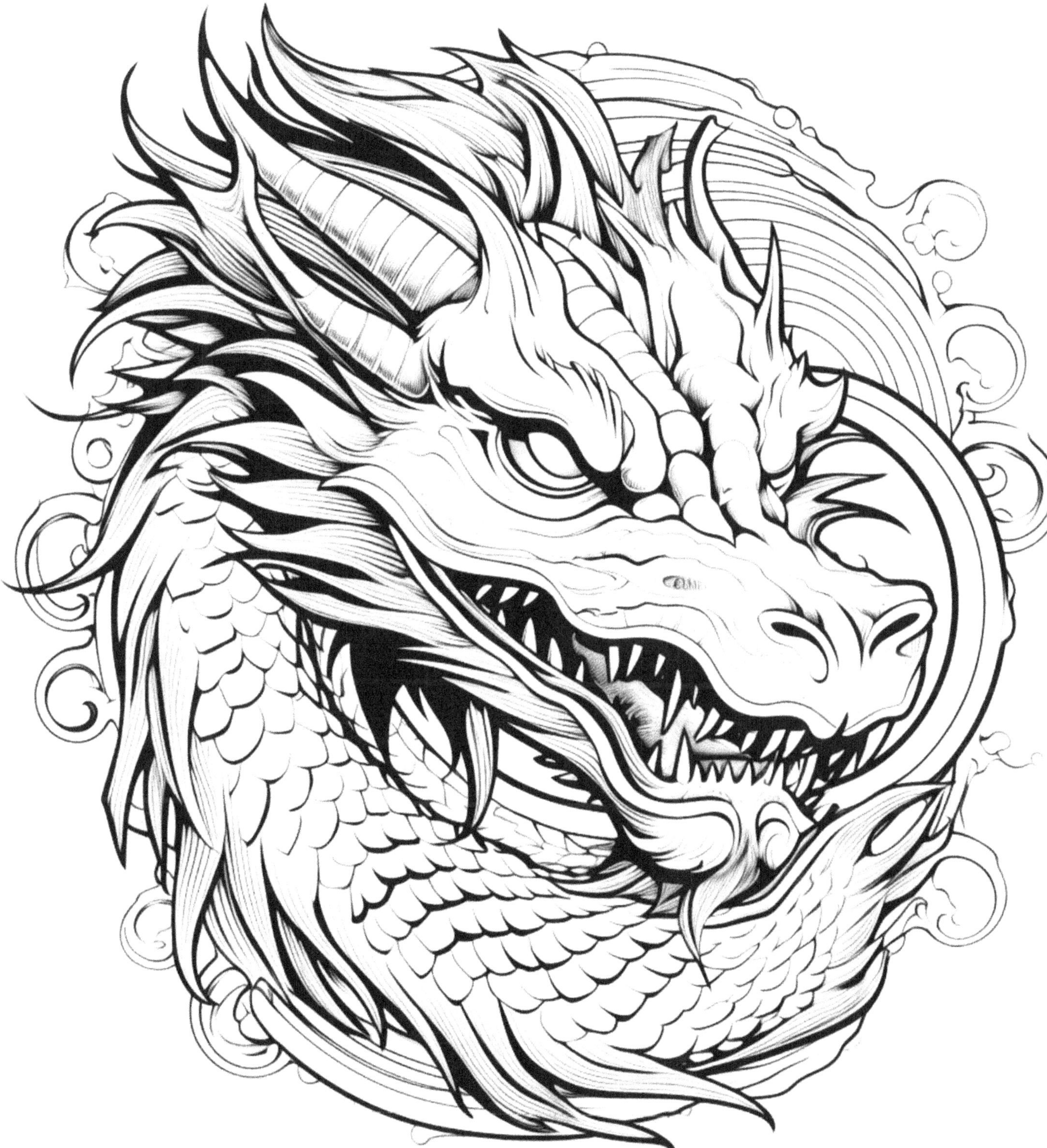

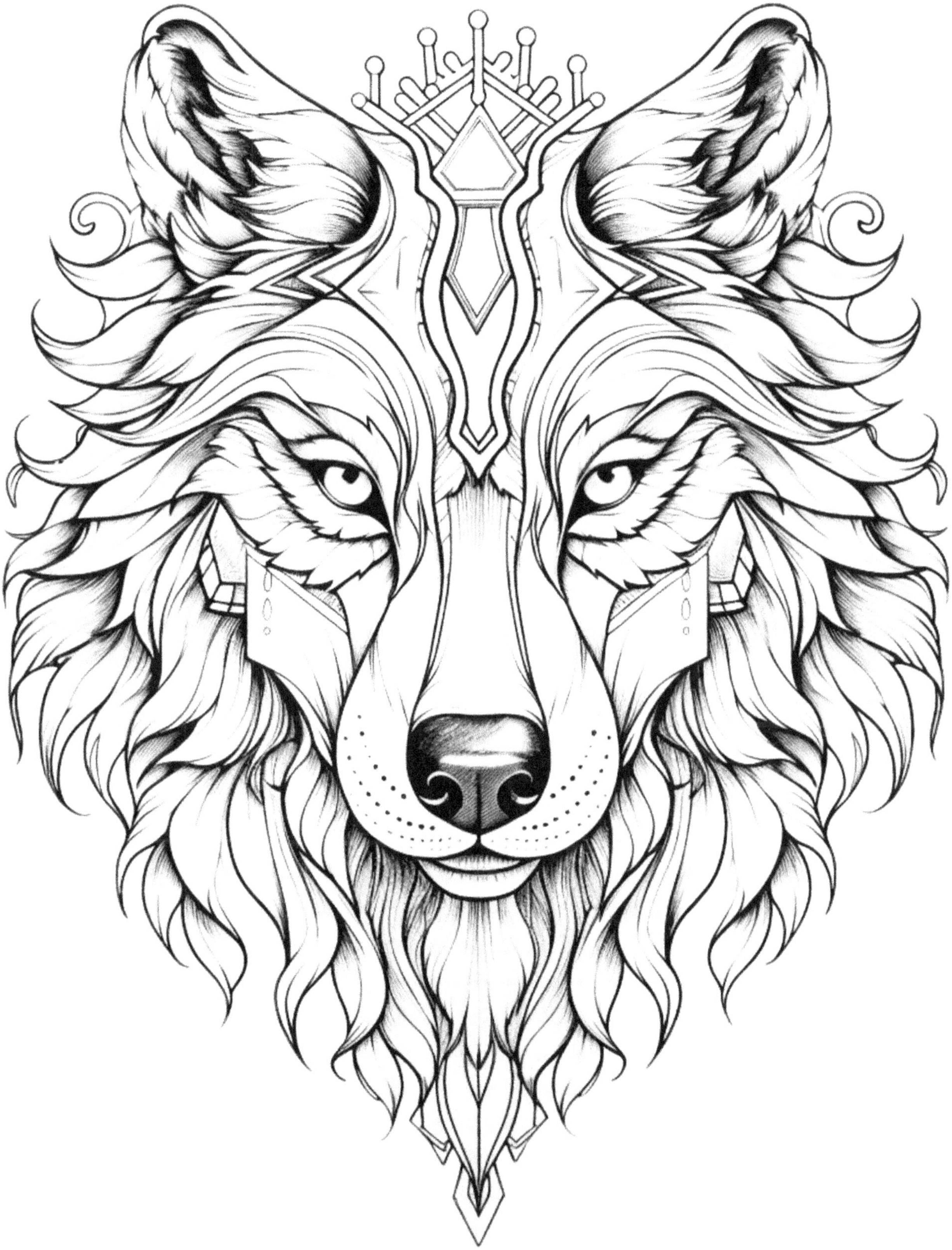

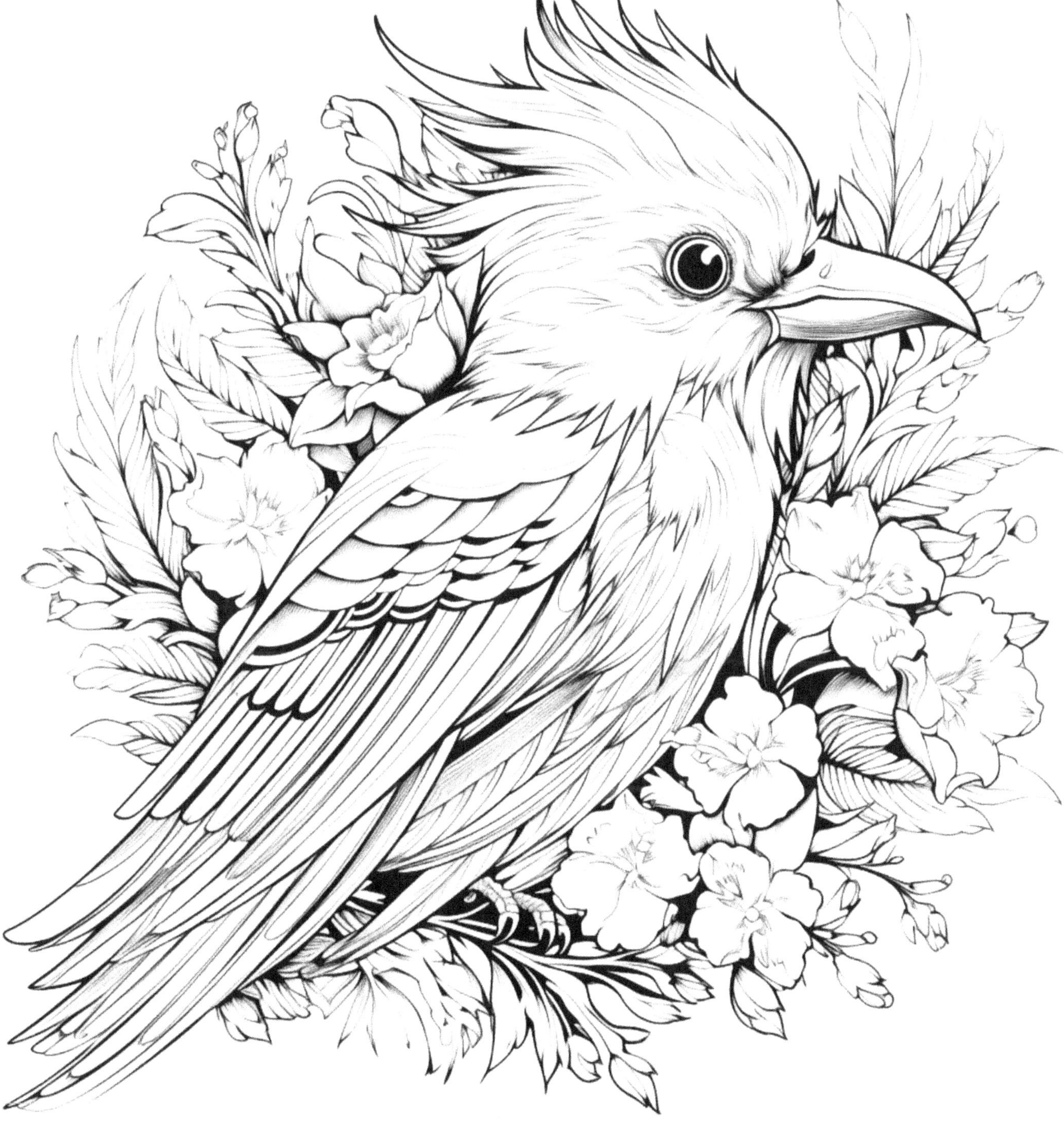

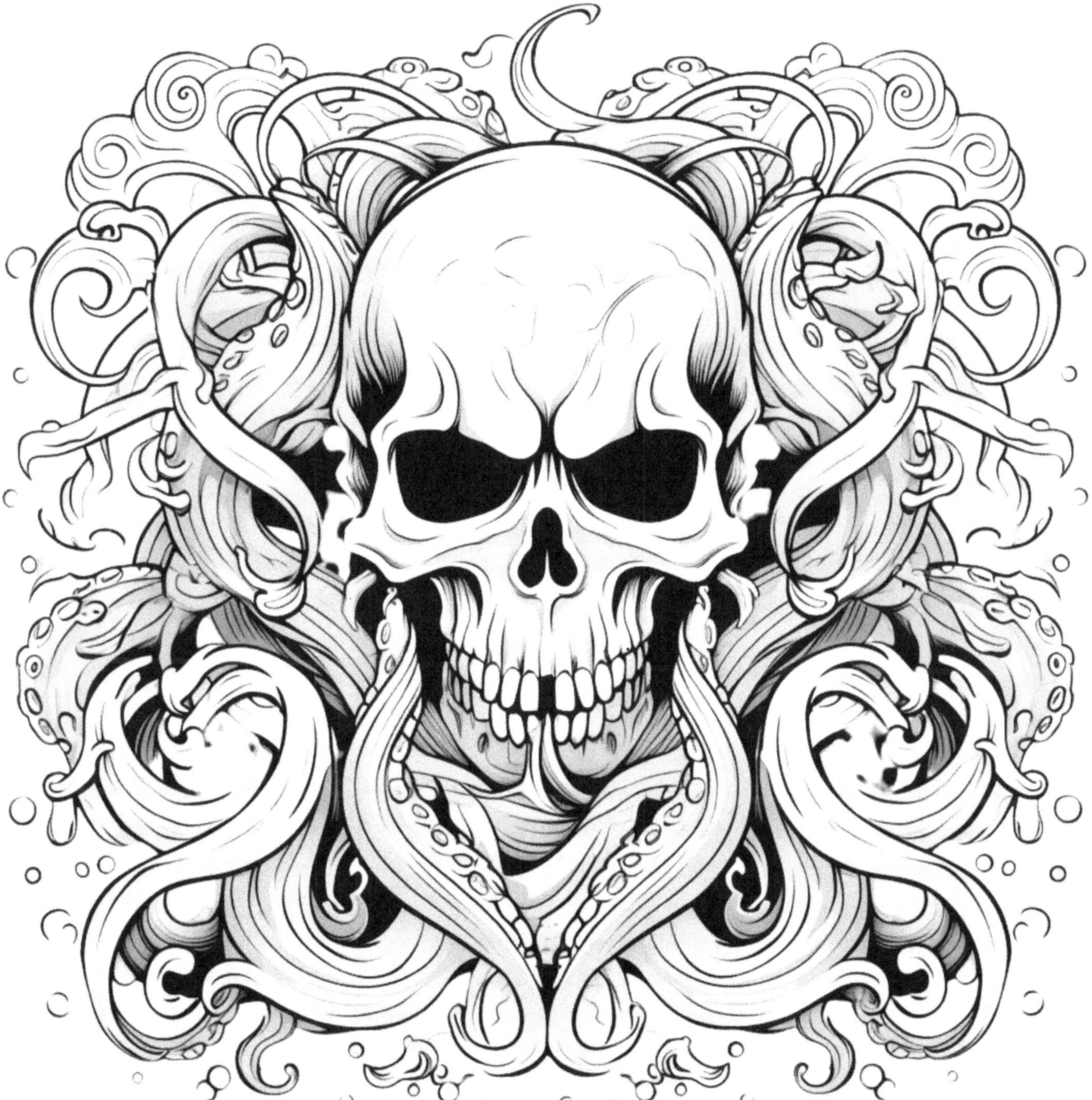

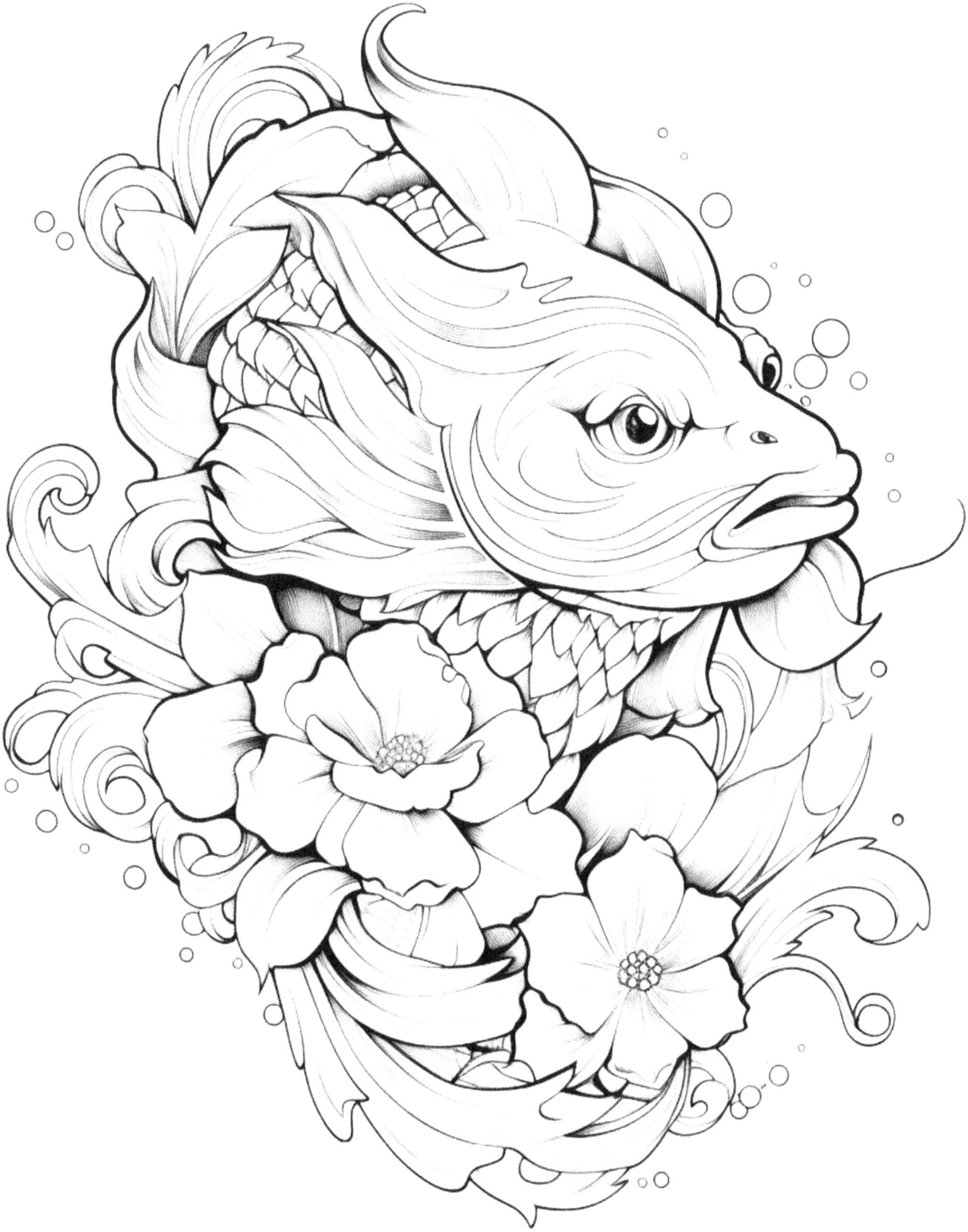

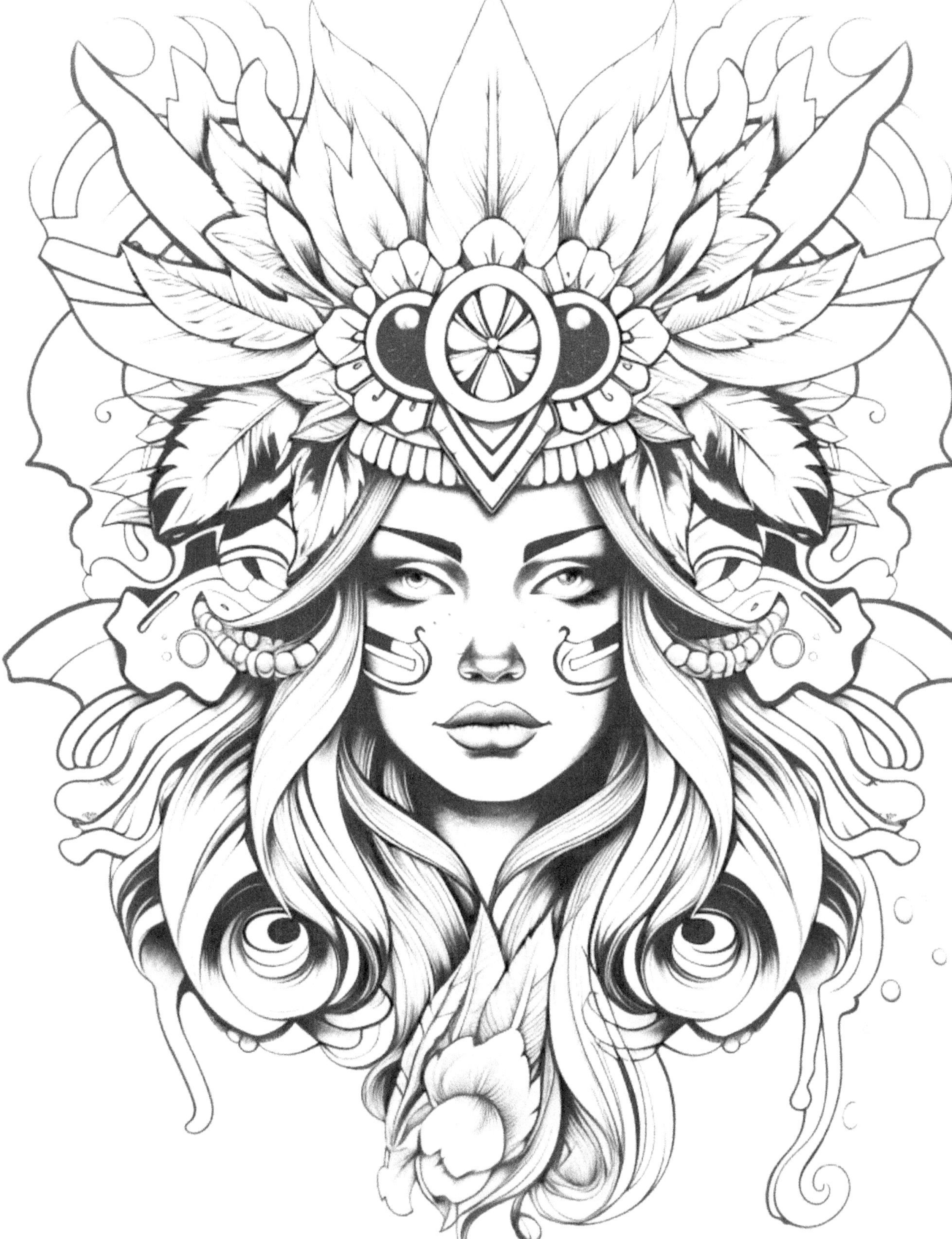

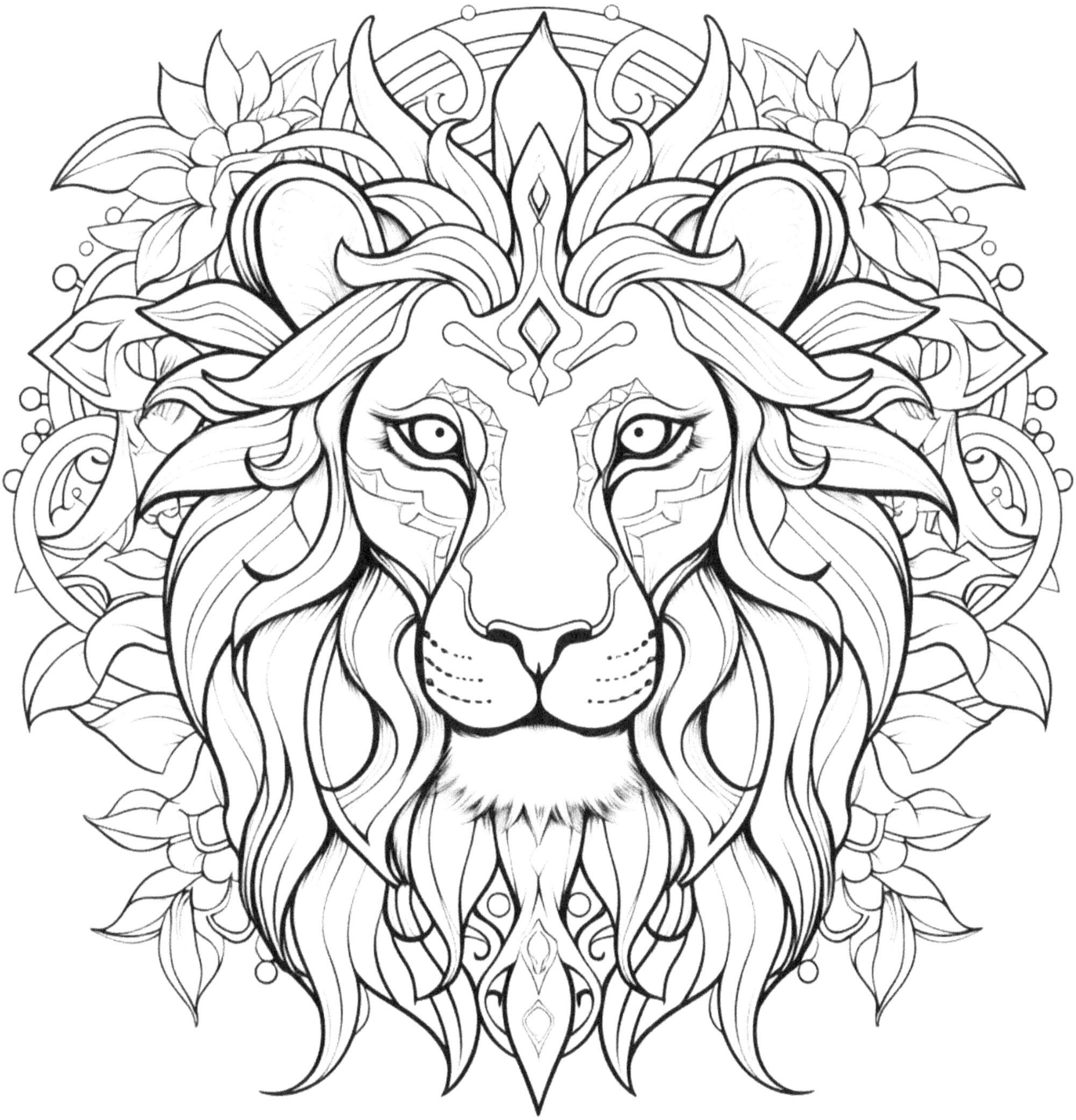

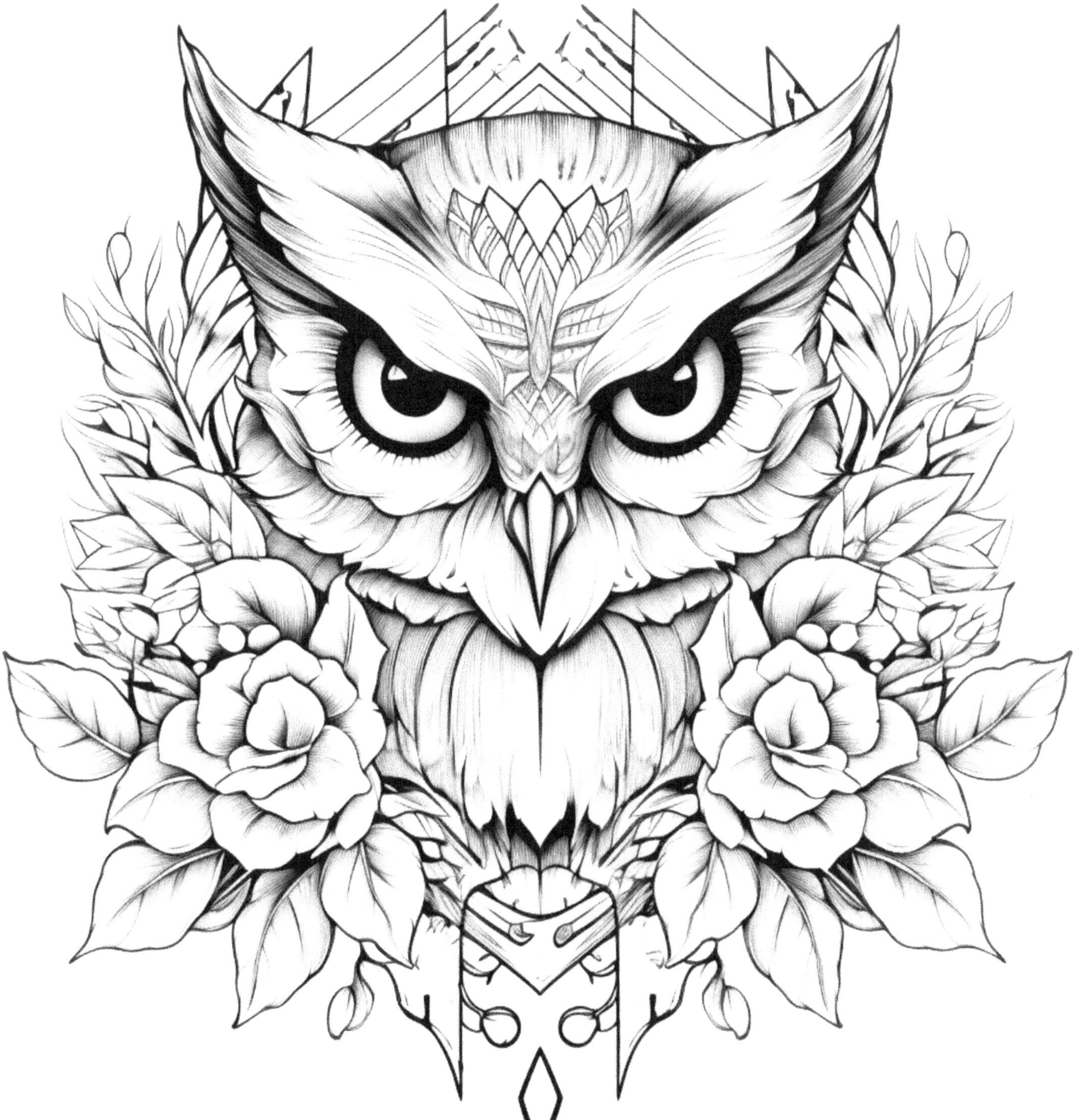

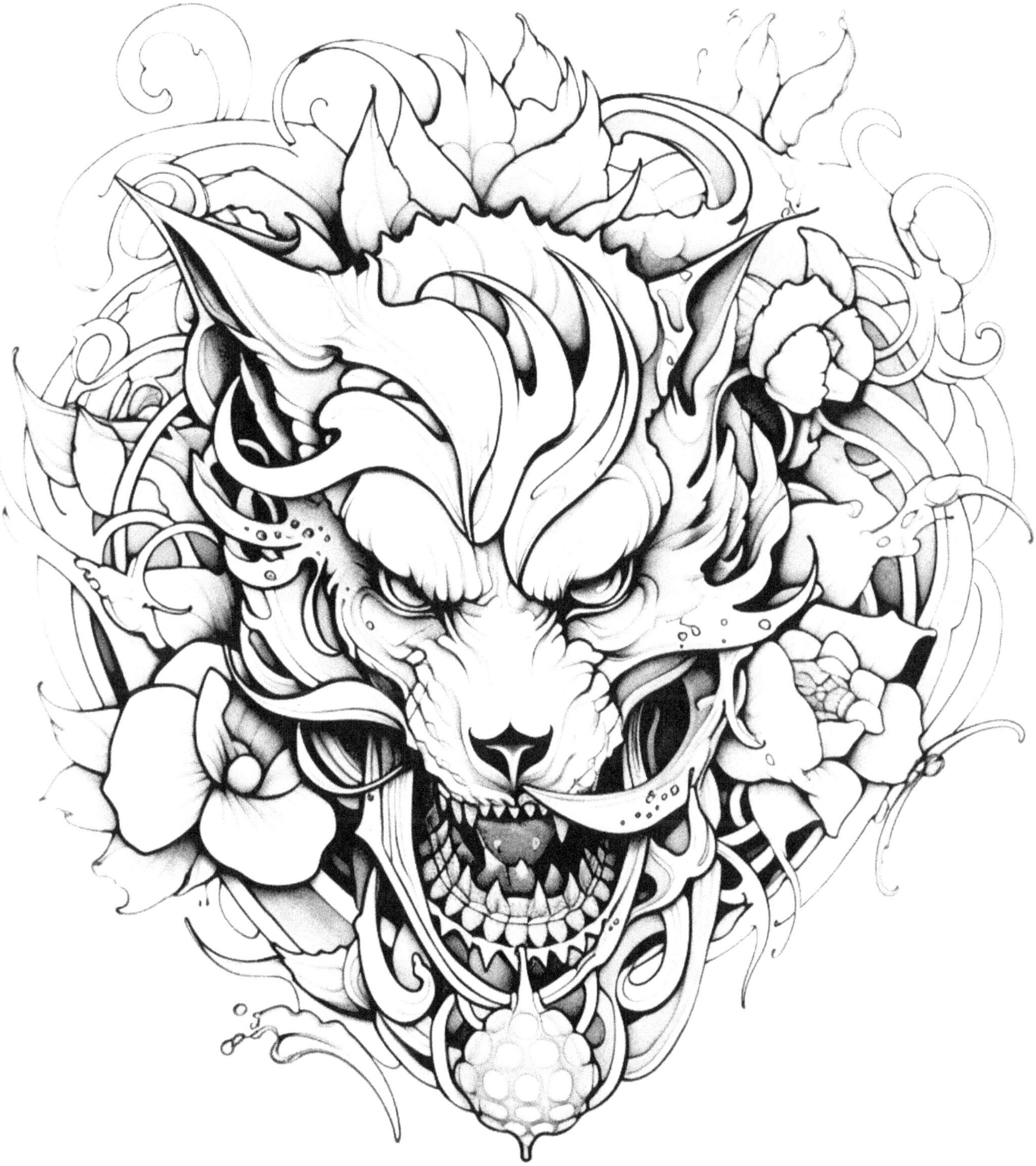

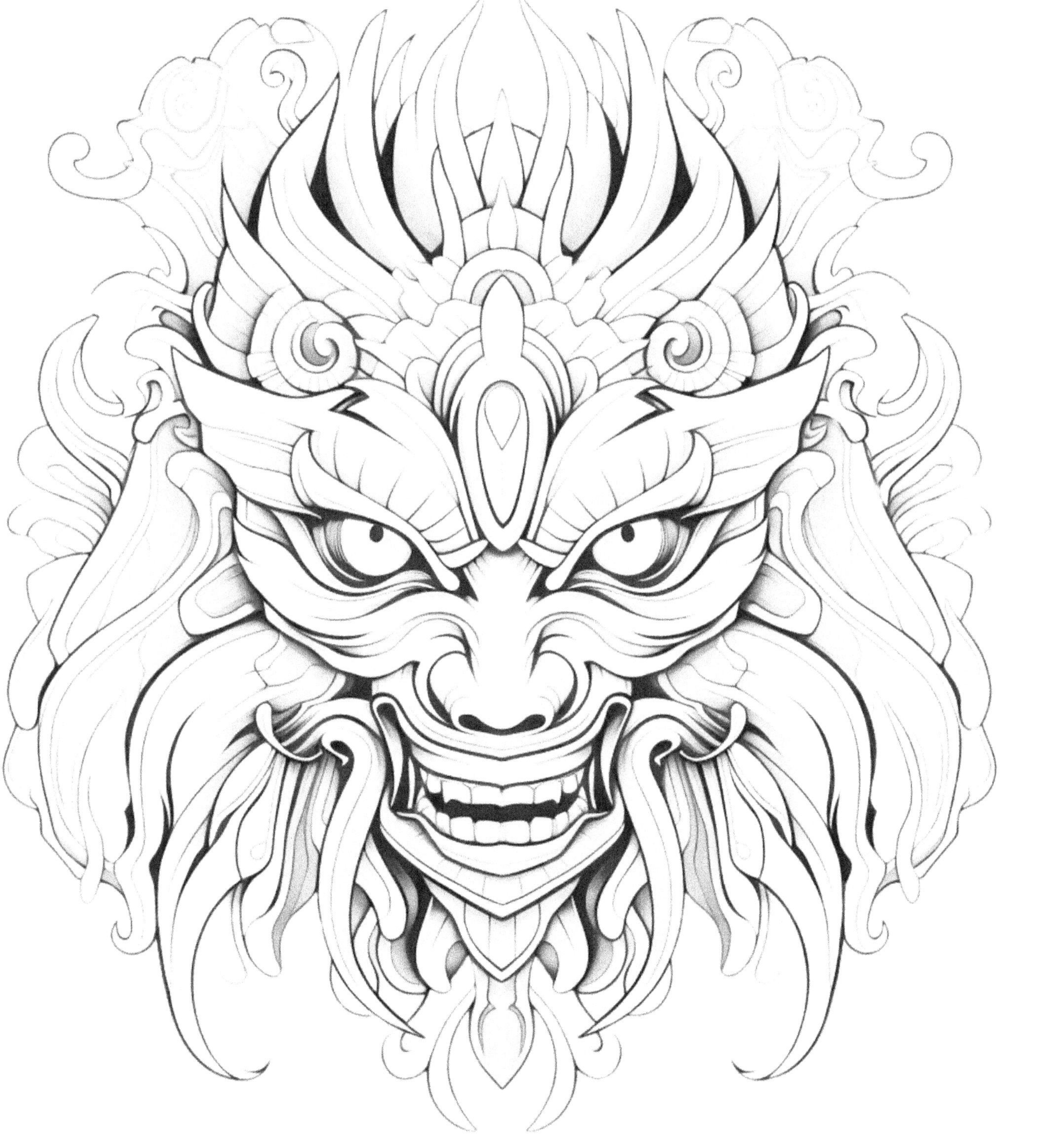

Traditional Tattoo

Coloring Book

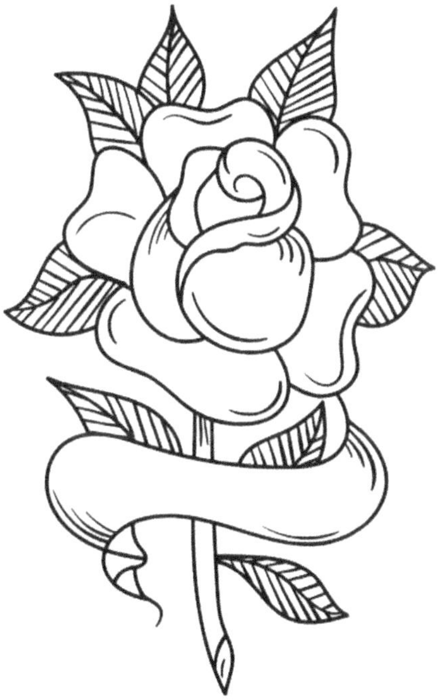

By Bruno Rodriguez

www.ingramcontent.com/pod-product-compliance
Lightning Source LLC
Chambersburg PA
CBHW082206290526
45794CB00008B/3445
* 9 7 9 8 8 6 6 3 9 1 4 9 3 *